# How to A

## Analyze Anyone Instantly:

*The Best Techniques to Read People like a Book for Increased Influence and Instant Social Leverage*

**Thank you and congratulations** for picking up *How to Analyze People: Analyze Anyone Instantly: The Best Techniques to Read People Like a Book for Increased Influence and Instant Social Leverage!*

You are on your way to increasing your social skills and improving your personal relationships with these powerful yet easy-to-follow, actionable strategies detailing how to analyze people effectively.

By purchasing this book, you have already shown that you are willing to take action and do what it takes to build an extraordinary life.

Don't forget to subscribe to the Modern Psychology Publishing newsletter, where you will be the first to receive information about new book releases, free promotions, and the latest news to help guide you on your journey of mastering your psychology!

In this book, you will learn:

✓ A reliable system for discovering personality type accurately - without them knowing!

✓ How to uncover psychological traits based on a framework of observation

✓ The best way to master body language and nonverbal cues

✓ The benefits of being able to analyze people effectively, and how it can lead to greater social influence

✓ How to determine if someone is lying

✓ And much, much more!

Let's get started!

of the recipient reader. Under no circumstances will any legal responsibility or blame be held against the publisher for any reparation, damages, or monetary loss due to the information herein, either directly or indirectly.

Respective authors own all copyrights not held by the publisher.

The information herein is offered for informational purposes solely, and is universal as so. The presentation of the information is without contract or any type of guarantee assurance.

The trademarks that are used are without any consent, and the publication of the trademark is without permission or backing by the trademark owner. All trademarks and brands within this book are for clarifying purposes only and are the owned by the owners themselves, not affiliated with this document.

# Table of Contents

# Introduction

**"Seeing the small is insight"**

*-Lao Tzu, Taoist and Philosopher*

The ability to analyze people can benefit you in a number of ways.

By studying someone, you get the advantage of knowing that person's feelings, emotions, and attitude even before the person utters a single word.

Moreover, the ability to analyze people helps you understand what the other person is going through. With this understanding, you can become empathetic (if the situation calls for empathy) and know what to do to make the person feel comfortable. This not only makes you likeable, it also fosters trusting relationships with those around you. When people trust you, influencing them becomes easier.

You can also use your 'people analysis' skill to manipulate people and subconsciously compel them to do as you please.

When you know what is going on in another person's head/mind, you can use that information to your advantage and tactfully persuade that person. Psychiatrists and detectives commonly use this skill to study and decipher individuals with ease.

Analyzing people also comes in handy in numerous situations. For example, if you are on a date, but your date constantly touching her face and avoids eye contact when you ask her a personal question, she is either telling you she is not interested, is thinking about something else, or may even be lying. By analyzing your date's body language, you easily understand what she is trying to communicate to you.

Or, let's say your aim is to get a raise from your boss. Wouldn't you will be much more likely to persuade him if you have an understanding of his values and decision making process? Perhaps your goal is to ask a stubborn coworker to help you on a project. How are you to know how to appeal to their sense of sociability if you don't understand their personality?

You simply cannot underestimate the value of knowing how to analyze people effectively.

Unfortunately, most people go through life not anticipating the importance of this skill and miss out on the opportunities and social leverage it can afford. Additionally, even if they know how to make observations about body language, typically people do not have a strategy for interpreting the information, and therefore can't benefit from really understanding the psychology behind someone's words and actions.

The solution is to develop a habit of becoming aware of what people are really communicating to you - understanding that most people do not explain their thought processes outright, and you have to do some interpretation.

The good new is, simply by having an interest in learning how to analyze people, you will find yourself becoming more observant about other people's actions and what they are really saying when you read between the lines.

Analysis comes down to 2 important elements: **Observation** and **Interpretation**.

**Observation** of body language and non-verbal cues is important to master, as humans speak more through their eyes and bodily gestures than actual words. If you can decipher the meaning locked in expressions, body language, and gestures, you can better understand what they are really communicating, both consciously and unconsciously. In the second part of this book, we will cover overall body language cues, speech pattern recognition and the basics of lie detection, an essential skill.

**Interpretation** is about using the knowledge gained through careful observation to derive gain an increased awareness of a person's thoughts, feelings, and general behaviours. In this book we will cover several personality analysis systems that will aid you to determining a person's behaviour and give you an accurate picture of their motivations.

By using the information gained from newfound observational skills, as well as you ability to determine personality types, you will develop a framework for being able to analyze and read people quickly and easily.

# Determining Personality Type

To be successful at analyzing people, you have to approach the seemingly nebulous factor of 'personality' in a very scientific way. The first thing we want to take note of is the fact that people people tend to fall into different personality categories based on their different mindset, how they act, and perceive things. Imagine that people are like computers: Determining personality based on type is a bit like figuring out which 'program' someone is running.

As stated before, people who share the same thoughts and ideas often appear to have a similar personality. For example, if you and your friend both enjoy each moment as it comes and stay in the moment and, it means you and your friend have a 'perceptive' personality and are likely to share similar thoughts in other areas of life as well.

To determine your target's exact personality, there are several systems of personality analysis which you can study in depth. The type of system you use depends on why you are trying to analyze someone. For instance, if you are an employer trying to analyze a potential hire capable for the job based on abilities, then you might want to use the DISC system.

## DISC System

DISC is a personal assessment tool used by over a million people to improve work productivity, teamwork, and ability to communicate. DISC stands for _dominance_, _influence_, _steadiness_, and _conscientiousness_.

The DISC system is an online personality assessment you can use to analyze your personality type. It consists of an electronic questionnaire that has questions with various options where you select the option that suits you the most.

The DISC system is best if you wish to analyze your abilities based on teamwork, examine how well you can handle stress, and manage a group of employees. To learn more about your personality using the DISC system you can visit www.discprofile.com.

Take the test first, to see where you fall. This will give you a framework for being able to analyze others and make sense of their personality with this system. When you have taken the test, you will notice that your personality is broken down into percentages of each component:

Dominance: People with a high Dominance factor tend to have strong personalities, good leadership skills, and value personal independence. They are determined and confident and often results oriented. However, they may lack patience and their big picture approach may mean they sometimes lack the ability to follow through on projects down to the details.

Influence: People in this category are interested in relationships. They are great at collaborating with others, and are motivated by social recognition and can easily influence and persuade others. They are warm, sociable and magnetic, and often popular. However, they can sometimes lack the ability to stay focused on a task and follow through completely.

Steadiness: This type is hardworking and consistent. They are detail oriented and they are focused on personal accomplishments. They value group acceptance, and may seek leadership through formal positions of authority. However, they are sometimes slow to adapt to new circumstances and tend to avoid change.

Conscientiousness: People with a high percentage of this factor are motivated by quality of work, and operate within existing circumstances to achieve the best possible result. They are consistent workers, and follow through on their work, valuing both accuracy and tact. However, they may need to learn how to become better at social collaboration and make an effort to participate more in group activities.

These are the four types within the DISC system. Your score will be an amalgamation of different percentages of each one, showing you which types you tend to exhibit most. For instance, you may have high Dominance and low Steadiness; which would mean you like to take control of situations, but may have trouble following through on small details. Understanding these things about yourself will allow you to become a better team player. In addition, being able to organize people into these categories will allow you insight and greater control over group dynamics.

While the DISC system is very good for understanding team dynamics and workplace scenarios, you can use other personality analysis systems to determine personality from a broader perspective. One such system is the Myers Briggs system.

# Myers Briggs Personality Analysis System

This system is the most reliable analysis system that gives very accurate results. The Myers and Briggs system bases its results on four dichotomies (Introverts vs Extroverts, Intuition vs Sensing, Thinking vs Feeling, and Judging vs Perceiving) making 16 possible combinations of personality.

Of course, similar to the DISC system, no one will be a perfect match to their Myers-Briggs personality type because every individual will have different experiences that shape who he or she is. (We will get into that very specific analysis in the next section). However, the Myers-Briggs system will provide a helpful framework that will help you uncover the intricacies of others' personalities.

The great thing about this system is that it is not necessary to have a person sit down and take the test so you can determine their personality type. Rather, there are ways you can covertly analyze your target and therefore determine (with great accuracy) where your target falls in the personality spectrum.

While this system takes a bit of effort to use, its insight into analyzing people is invaluable. Furthermore, the more comfortable you get at identifying the personality types as detailed in this system, it will be easier to analyze someone the next time you wish to do so. Again, you may also wish to take this test for yourself so you can have a frame of reference as you seek to understand the different personality types.

Using this system to covertly analyze people is simple. Simply determine where they fall in each of the 4 dichotomies (Introverts vs Extroverts, Intuition vs Sensing, Thinking vs Feeling, Judging vs Perceiving). Once you have this information, you will have a four letter combination such as INTJ. Using this code, look up their personality type and read all about them, without them even knowing!

Once you use this system to determine your target's four characteristics, you can determine a great deal of information about who the person is and what motivates him or her as a person.

## Introvert (I) vs. Extrovert (E)

Introverts are likely to be hesitant; they avoid social interactions, are generally withdrawn or cautions, and keep their thoughts and feelings to themselves. On the other hand, Extroverts are very interactive and utilize energy from the outer world. They are easily adaptable and confidently deal with and enjoy social situations. Extroverts are often the life of the party, but on the other hand they need other people to thrive.

Let's look at an example. If your friend avoids meeting people, likes sitting in a quiet place, and hardly shares what is on her mind, that friend is most likely an introvert. An extremely introverted person's body language shows rigidity in public. They may avoid going to crowded areas and try to find a quiet place to chill out. They are most comfortable when spending time alone rather than attending parties. Even in social gathering, introverts may tend to avoid physical contact or involvement in long conversations with new people.

Introverts keep their body language closed and talk in a soft tone to avoid attention. For instance, when you try to engage someone in conversation and suddenly, he/she stiffens, starts avoiding eye contact and talks quickly in order to cut short the conversation, by observing these signs, you will easily identify the person you are talking to as an Introvert.

Extroverts are the complete opposites. They like getting involved in conversations and like being around people. They talk more to keep the conversation going and exhibit many gestures as they talk. They like drawing attention to themselves.

Next time you are analyzing someone, first make observations to determine whether that person is an Introvert (I) or an Extrovert (E). Then, move on to the next personality factor.

## Sensing vs. Intuition

Intuition is the natural ability that allows you to know about something without tangible proof. Intuition helps you sense something wrong or good to come ahead. People with a strong intuition trust their sixth sense and gut feeling to explore data more deeply rather than a Sensing type.

Intuitive people are future oriented and believe in being innovative rather than following traditional trends. People who believe in their intuition make decisions by being fully aware of the consequences ahead. They find different solutions to solve a problem by trusting their instinct. For instance, whenever and Intuitive type encounters a challenge, they may use their sixth sense and intuition to make an informed decision. They may close their eyes, analyze the difficult situation in my head, and try to tap into their intuitive side to find an appropriate solution to the problem. Instead of logically analyzing the situation and rummaging through data, they go with a gut feeling.

On the other hand, people with a strong sensory ability believe only what they see and experience. They make decisions with a conscious mind instead of trusting their subconscious mind. Sensors limit themselves to data and do not think beyond what can be tangibly proven.

They believe in logic rather than trusting their sixth sense. They focus more on what is practical and closer to reality. However they may tend to follow the trodden path instead of finding new possibilities and ways.

How someone uses language (words) can easily help you analyze if a person is an intuitive type or sensing type. Intuitive people always make things about themselves. If facing a problem, they use their ideas and experiences to find a solution. In a conversation, they will say "I believe, I feel, I think, or in my opinion," quite often.

Sensing types however, start and end conversations with logic. They avoid repetition and do not give personal real life examples until asked.

So is the person you are analyzing a Sensing type (S), or an Intuitive type (N)? Once you have this letter determined, move on to the next section.

## Thinking vs. Feeling

This dichotomy refers to how people make decisions.

Thinkers make decisions based on a fact or a principle. They analyze the pros and cons and make logical decisions. They make decisions using their brain instead of listening to their hearts. They always look for logical solutions and explanations. While making decisions, thinkers can be very impersonal, and try to not let their emotions cloud their judgement. They like to see the basic truths involved, rather than relying on what others feel.

As opposed to this, those driven by emotions and feelings value these two elements more than logical thought and reasoning. If you make decisions keeping in mind the views and sentiments of other people involved in a situation, it means you value feelings more than logical reasoning and belong to the 'feeling' category.

Take a moment to think about the person you are analyzing again. Do you think they are a Thinking (T) type, or more of a Feeling, (F) type? When they make decisions, do they do it based on facts and logic, or are they more concerned about the emotions of others and value tact over complete honesty?

## Judging vs. Perceiving

Someone who has a Judging style or personality is well prepared for the outer world. Such people are well-organized, good planners, and to avoid stress, give their best in every aspect. They believe in doing work beforehand and work best before meeting deadlines. They can sometimes have more of a rigid body language, fast gait, and narrowed eyebrows showing their concern regarding work.

On the other hand, someone with a Perceiving personality is more flexible at adapting to new changes compared to someone with a Judging personality. Because they have a strong self-belief, the perceiving types are comfortable making decisions without any specific plans and are good at multi-tasking. They avoid involving themselves in activities that drive them away from their freedom of experimenting.

Someone who has a Perceiving personality will have a relaxed body posture with high spirit. He or she will believe in having light conversations, allowing others to share their ideas, and tend not to engage in stressful conversations regarding work. They challenge the stress instead of letting it challenge them.

So is the person you are analyzing more of a Judging (J) type or a Perceiving (P) type? Do they approach life as if it were a checklist of accomplishments, or are they more easy going and apt to freestyle, not completely sure of their next move?

Now that you have identified the four dimensions of personality as displayed by your target, you can look up their personality type online, and read a full summary of their personality profile. One great website you can use is www.16personalities.com. So, if you have determined that your target is likely Extrovert (E), Intuitive (I), Feeling (F), and Judging (J), read the profile of an ENFJ, 'The Protagonist' to get a sense of his or her personality in detail.

Keep in mind, of course, that more analysis will need to be done to further understand the person through their life unique experience.  Let us now go a step further and learn about individual analysis.

# Individual Analysis

Despite the reliability of the Myers-Briggs test, we know that all people are going to be highly individual in how they express their personality types. Not everyone in a certain personality type is going to be the same in terms of ways of how they act, what they are motivated by, etc.

Many factors in a person's life experience influence a person's specific personality. This can be confusing if you do not know where to look. However, there are a couple key things that when determined, will allow us great clarity into your target's individual personality.

Using what you learned about personality type, you can apply these principles to uncover more information about your target's true individual personality. You can also gain a great deal of information about these things through conversation while of course, framing your questions in a politely curious way, rather than asking questions that may be too personal. Here, you will have to use your judgment to determine the best way to extract detailed information from your target.

To better analyze someone, you need to be aware of that person's perceived strengths and weaknesses. Let us find out what these are.

## Perceived Strengths

Your perceived strengths are the qualities and strengths you want people to see in you. For instance, if you are good at dancing and are a humble person, you exhibit your dance skills in front of people and are always humble because that is how you want people to see you.

Similarly, your target has some perceived strengths. Knowing your target's strengths helps you encourage and boost your target's confidence. This helps you easily communicate with and influence them.

For instance, if you meet someone whose biggest strength is designing clothes, you can boost that person's confidence by appreciating his or her work and giving him or her the confidence to exhibit his/her talent to the world. This will cause the person to like you and gradually consider you a confidant worth listening to simply because you admired the person's personal prowess.

To determine your target's perceived strengths, spend time with the target; analyze what he or she is good at, how he or she sees him or herself, and how he or she wants the world to perceive him/her.

For instance, if your brother constantly talks about how helpful he is to his friends, it means he wants people to perceive him as a helpful person. If your father never stops talking about his bravery, it means he wants you to perceive him as a bold and courageous person.

In addition to analyzing your target's strengths, you also need to understand his or her weaknesses. Let us explore this further:

## Perceived Weaknesses

Your perceived weaknesses are the shortcomings you want to hide from the world or shortcomings you feel the need to compensate for or be compensated for. Similarly, the people you wish to analyze has some perceived weaknesses.

For instance, if your best friend is has a habit of using marijuana, but tries to hide it from the people who respect him, it means he is not proud of his perceived weakness.

For varied reasons, it is important to be aware of your target's perceived weaknesses. First, it allows you a chance to help your target get better or overcome weaknesses, thus causing the target to trust you, which then makes persuading such a person easier.

Secondly, knowing your target's perceived weaknesses helps you influence that person and cause him or her to pay heed to your advice in certain situations. For instance, if your marijuana-addicted friend refuses to lend you his car, you may understand that it is because he does not want others to know of his habit, not because he doesn't trust you with his car.

Moreover, it is also important to know of your target's primary motivations.

## Primary Motivations

Another important factor that helps you understand people well is their primary motivation(s). Primary motivations are the ultimate desires, ambitions, and wishes that drive your behavior and influence you. For instance, if you are passionate about singing, your primary motivation is singing since you aspire to become a renowned international singer.

To get better insight into people, you need to know about their primary motivations so you can know what drives and inspires them. Your target's perceived strengths and weaknesses help you understand the target's primary motivations.

A person's perceived strengths and weaknesses often serve as the motivating factors behind that person's primary motivations.

For example, if someone wants others to perceive him as a generous person, then he will give donations and collect funds for helpless people. On the other hand, someone perceived as being poor may aspire to become incredibly rich at some point in his or her life.

Additionally, look for your target's fears. This will mostly relate to your target's perceived weaknesses. Your target's fears help you know what scares him/her so you can use that information to improve your communications.

If you want to improve the target's self-confidence, you can help him/her move past his fears. For example, if your sister lacks confidence, she may be scared of speaking publicly. If you see her behaving strangely in a crowd or in front of a complete stranger, you can easily identify her fear and will be better able to talk with her and give her the confidence she needs the next time she has to speak in front of people.

In addition to this information, knowing someone's birth order can help you to effectively analyze people.

## Birth Order

You may not think that birth order is of great importance in predicting the behavior of adults, but in fact, determining a target's birth order can yield great insight.

The role someone plays while growing up will continue to have an impact on how that person looks at the world even as the person grows to become an adult. The treatment accorded to you in your childhood determines your personality and your perception about yourself and of the world.

For instance, if you are the first child, it is likely you received the most attention from your parents, which is why you are more confident than the rest of your siblings. Let us study the characteristic of different birth orders so you can know how to dig a little more into your target's personality.

## First Child

During the birth of a first child, parents are more attentive and concerned about the child's health, upbringing, and the activities the child is involved in. The extra parental care and attention is likely to turn the first child into a 'perfectionist'. The following are the common characteristics that can help you identify firstborns:

- Firstborns are trusted to be very reliable because in their parent's eyes, they are perfect.
- Firstborns are highly motivated towards success.
- They like taking charge of the situation and try their best to please their parents.
- They are highly confident and determined.
- Their body language is mostly strong and shows their self-belief.

## Second Child (Middle Child)

Most parents raise their second child in a more relaxed manner. The attention given to the second child competes with that given to the first child. Middle children are often the opposite of the first child.

The following are the common characteristic of the second child:

- Lack of attention given to the second child makes the child insecure and secretive.

- Second born children are attention seekers.

- They are more independent because they do not rely on their parents or elder siblings.

- They are rebellious and have "I have my own life" attitude.

- Second born children are peacemakers because their birth order allows them to see all sides of a situation.

## Last-Born

Last-born children or the youngest child in the family is the family's baby. The characteristic of the last-born children are as follows:

- They have a carefree attitude because they share no responsibility.

- They are spoiled and have chances to develop a rebellious personality because of the extra love given to them.

- Last-born children can lighten the atmosphere with their presence.

- They are likely to be stubborn thanks in part to the extra love and care they receive.

## Only Child

A singleton is an only child. Compared to children who have one or more siblings, singletons are likely to receive extra parental attention. Here are the basic characteristics of an only child.

- Their self-esteem and self-confidence levels are high because they receive undivided parental love and attention. This is visible through their confident gait, style of talking, and body language.
- Because they never had to share their belongings with anyone, they have a high sense of privacy. They may act a little private amongst other kids and may not easily settle in because they need more time and space to adjust to new surroundings.
- They are independent and enjoy doing things independently. They may also not be good team players. If you see someone, who does not adjust well to a group and demands to work alone, that person is most likely a singleton.

In addition to the birth order, a person's gender also influences his or her behavior, attitude, and thinking pattern. If someone is a second child male, he is likely to be more dominant than a female second born. Since males usually assume different roles in society and with their siblings, their behavior is different from their female counterparts.

If a second born male has an elder sister, he is still likely to be more confident and boisterous than his sister.

Hence, whenever you analyze a person, also consider the person's birth order and gender.

## Belief Systems

Religious and spiritual beliefs are certainly an important factor, but the term 'belief system' refers to a broader range of possibilities. This is about determining the *framework* that someone has for ordering his or her life experiences.

Each of us has a different belief system based on what we think 'makes sense' or has some 'logic'. The life experiences we go through greatly influence how we build our belief systems.

For example, your best friend strongly believes being a failure does not make you a loser. This is so because he never looked back at his failure and instead, worked harder to attain his goals. The experience one goes through greatly influence that person's belief systems.

Beliefs often determine what is possible as well as what someone is likely to achieve. The best show of this is the famous anecdotal story of the first 1954 4-minute mile run by Roger Bannister.

Before that record-breaking event, the populace (even seasoned runners) believed it was impossible to run a 4-minute mile. Part of Roger's training involved rigorous visualization of the certainty that running a mile in under 4-minutes was indeed possible.

After Roger broke that record, many runners all of a sudden started running a mile in under 4 minutes. Roger Bannister's historic run changed many people's belief systems and helped them turn their negative beliefs into positive ones.

All the life experiences we go through have a different impact on our belief system based on our life experiences. How you (or someone else) perceives the world depends upon the treatment given to him by the world.

For instance, if you meet someone who is full of positive energy, someone who is ready to accept challenges and believes in spreading love, this person's positive attitude tells you his/her belief system is about a happy and peaceful world.

On the other hand, if you meet a person who is not confident and avoids social interactions, you will pick up clues of the person having bad experiences that shattered his self-belief.

Your target's beliefs give you a deeper understanding of the target's thought process. What the target believes in clearly tells you how he or she perceives the world. For instance, if your brother believes in his abilities, he is likely to behave confidently, talk assertively, and always take responsibility for tasks assigned to him.

On the other hand, if your cousin always complains of how unfair life is, is seldom happy, and always acts as the victim in a challenging situation, his demeanor helps you understand he has a negative belief system.

In addition to understanding your target's general belief system, also seek to gain insight into the target's core beliefs, limiting beliefs, and other beliefs such as social, economic, religious, and political beliefs because understanding these things will help you understand the person that much better.

## Core Beliefs

Core beliefs are the beliefs we truly believe in; they help us set the principles we base how we live our lives on. For instance, a core belief could be honesty and sincerity; if a person is always honest and sincere in their professional and personal dealings with people they have a strong value system that determines how they act.

You can determine someone's core belief through his or her speech and his/her outlook on the outer world. If you meet someone who very enthusiastically talks about how happy he is to help people and the appreciation he gets from others, you can conclude that this person's core belief is to become a better person and spread positivity.

## Limiting Beliefs

Limiting beliefs are the negative thoughts that stop you from attaining your full potential. For instance, if you believe you cannot be a better person, then that belief is your limiting belief.

You can identify someone's limiting beliefs by spending time with the person and talking about how he or she views him or herself and life in general. If you are talking to someone who talks about his passion of becoming a writer but is holding back his talent because he fears he cannot become a good writer, it clearly shows he nurtures a limiting belief about his potential.

## Other Beliefs

We have many other beliefs such as religious, political, economic, and social beliefs. Covertly research and interrogate your target's other beliefs so you can know what things he or she believes in.

For instance, if your friend practices Hinduism and is strictly religious, you know you should not say anything against the religion in front of him.

Additionally, it is also important to pay attention to your target's unconscious triggers.

## Unconscious Triggers

Unconscious triggers are the stimuli that unconsciously affect us without our awareness. For instance, if someone loses their temper if someone mentions politics, it may be one of their unconscious stress triggers.

Similarly, each of us has some triggers that trigger different emotions without our awareness. Everyone has experienced life events that have produced great emotional reactions. Sometimes even word/s will trigger a strong reaction in a person if the word/s strongly ties to a memory.

To analyze people, take note of their unconscious triggers so you can determine what makes them happy, sad, upset, and feel other emotions. To do that, spend time with your target and be attentive to his or her emotions.

If you notice the target's happy expression changing to a sad one, focus on what happened in that moment. Did someone say something upsetting? Did the target eat something terrible? Did he or she experience an emotional trauma? Examining such things helps you know your target's unconscious triggers so you can use those triggers to influence your target.

Now that we have identified these key areas of insight, we have a very good understanding of who the target is as a person. By practicing these observation techniques, you will be in a position to analyze people more accurately.

When analyzing someone, one important thing you should remember is to have an open mind and not let your judgment and perceptions cloud your analysis.

# Building Blocks Of Analysis: Understanding Body Language

Now that we have a framework for understanding personality, let's discuss how to increase our powers of observation.

The best way to analyze people is by keenly observing the signals they transmit non-verbally. If we carefully observe people in any social situation, (for instance at a party, a romantic dinner, or in a job interview), we become aware that they are continuously broadcasting hundreds of signals to us every second through their body language, speech patterns, and unconscious gestures. Our subconscious picks up on all of these signals; however, not all of this information can possibly be processed by our conscious mind.

According to research conducted by UCLA, only 7% of our communication with others consists of the words we actually say. The rest of the conversation, a whopping 93%, consists of body language and the tone of your speech with body language comprising of 55% and tone accounting for around 38%of the conversation.

42

By understanding body language and tone variations, you can easily read people. To gain a deeper understanding of this concept, we need to look at a few examples:

Imagine one of your female friends is clinically depressed. When you meet your friend, you focus more on her words than her body posture. Later, upon recalling the conversation, you start to remember that her hands were shaking and she failed to maintain direct eye contact. In such an instance, Focusing on her body language helps you understand how bad her depressive state is.

Here is another instance; while you and your elder brother are discussing politics, you see him crossing his arms in front of his chest. While you may not understand the coded message in this gesture, your brother is simply trying to say that something you have said has offended him.

Your body language speaks volumes about what you feel and think. To analyze people, you need to get a better understanding of body language:

# Body Language

The common belief is that body language refers to your body posture only. While that notion has some truth to it, body language refers to unconscious and conscious body postures, movements, and gestures by which you communicate your feelings, emotions, and attitudes. It not only includes your posture, it also encompasses your facial expressions, eye contact, and movement of your arms and legs.

By observing someone's body language, you can easily understand the person's emotions without the need for verbal cues. To understand this, let us go through some common body postures and their meanings.

### Arms Crossed in Front of Chest

This gesture indicates the person you are talking to is being defensive or disagrees with you. For instance, if during a group discussion, you raise a point that contradicts with your friend's opinion and he stiffly crosses his arms around his chest, your friend is expressing disagreement

## Nail Biting

Nail biting shows nervousness, stress, or a state of confusion. People unconsciously bite their nails when tensed or nervous. This body language gesture is common in students sitting for an exam.

## Hands on Cheek

If someone is sitting with hand on cheek and furrowed eyebrows, it means the person is lost in thought. If you are talking to someone and the person makes this gesture, it means that person is not attentive and his or her attention is somewhere else.

For example, if you meet a friend who is sitting with his hand on his cheek, it means he is not concentrating on you and is thinking deeply about something else. Through keen observation, you can talk to your friend about what is bothering him, thus showing him your concern.

## Touching the Nose

If someone makes this gesture, it means the person is either lying to you or showing rejection and disbelief in some opinion.

In many conversations, people give signals of rejection by frequently rubbing their nose instead of directly talking about it.

Moreover, if someone is hiding something from you, or is lying about something, the person is likely to rub his or her nose too.

## Stroking the Chin

If someone makes this gesture, it means he/she is in deep thought or is busy deciding something. If you often see, your boss stroke his chin when thinking about an important business decision or otherwise, you now know what this gesture implies.

## Head Nodding

If someone makes this gesture while talking to you, it means he agrees with you. This submissive gesture tells you that you and your listener are on the same page. For example, if you have noticed your audiences nod their heads while you present a speech, it means they agreed with you.

If someone does not nod his or her head when conversing with you, it means the person disagrees with you or cannot understand your point.

In addition to these gestures, the eye contact people make with you communicates a lot about their hidden feelings. Let us dig deeper into different sorts of eye contact.

## Eye Contact

Eye contact is another signal that silently tells what the other person is feeling or hiding. Eyes indicate attention, interest, and your involvement with the next person. The length of eye contact, blinking of the eye, and pupil dilation are all cues of nonverbal communication

Let us find out what different types of eye contact mean.

### Lowered Gaze

If you are talking to someone and then the person lowers his or her gaze, it has two meanings: the person is lying or is feeling shy. For instance, if you date a person and your date finds it hard to maintain eye contact, smiles and lowers her gaze, this says she is feeling shy.

On the contrary, if you ask your friend a personal question and while answering, he avoids eye contact and has a blank or worried expression on his face, it means he is hiding the truth or is not comfortable sharing personal issues.

## Keeping Consistent Eye Contact

If you are talking to someone and he maintains direct eye contact without blinking or looking around, it means you have that person's full attention and he or she is fully involved in the conversation. Direct eye contact shows the level of confidence in your listener and the interest he/she has in the conversation.

## Glance (Conscious)

If someone sitting next to you breaks eye contact by looking downwards, it means he or she is attracted to you but is feeling shy. However, if he or she breaks eye contact by looking towards the sides, it means he/she is not interested in the conversation or in you.

Another important component of body language is your facial expressions. Let us explore a few common facial expressions and the meanings they hold.

## Facial Expressions

The Face is the medium through which we express human moods. Different facial expressions communicate different things. Here are a few common facial expressions we often use to express our emotions to others.

## Smile

Happiness is a universal expression easily observed through widened lips (smiling) and crescent shaped eyes. A smile identifies a person's happiness through his widened lips and crescent eyes.

## Crinkling of Eyes

When you smile, tiny crinkles form at the corners of the eye indicating genuine happiness. If you want to observe whether the person next to you is actually smiling or faking a smile, then look for the crinkles at the corner of the eye. This is the best way to analyze someone's genuine happiness or insincerity.

## Slanted Eyebrows

If someone has slanted eyebrows and a frown, then you can easily understand he is sad. The dullness of the eyes indicates sadness or defeat. People show such facial expressions when they are withdrawn and lack excitement.

## Widened Eyes and Eyebrows Slanted Upwards

If you are talking to someone whose eyebrows appear slanted upwards and eyes widened, it means the person is fearful of something. In a 2008 scientific study conducted to study the fearful face, researchers discovered that people who show fear by breathing air and widening their eyes could attract their target of fear towards them.

## Anger

The demeanor of an angry person is unmistakable. An angry person squeezes the eyebrows to form a crease and has tight and narrowed eyelids. The person cheeks turn red due to blood rushing through the body at a high speed and the person lowers his or her head.

If someone is angry with you, the person's facial expressions and body posture will be stiff.

### Lowering of Eyes

If you see someone lowering his eyes to avoid eye contact, has a worried expression on the face, and points his head downwards, it means they are ashamed of something.

### Pursed Lips and Narrowed Eyes

If you see your spouse's lips tightly pursed, eyes narrowed and eyebrows raised, it means she is confused about something.

## Gestures with Hands and Arms

You can also analyze people by observing the movements of their arms and hands. While communicating, people unconsciously use their arms and hands to make gestures. Hand gestures aid communication without verbal discussions. The following are the most commonly observed hand and arms gestures.

### Clenched Hands

Clenched hands represent negative attitude, giving you a signal of frustration or irritation. We clench hands in three common ways: hands clenched in raised position, hands clenched in middle position, and hands clenched in low position. All three types represent negative moods.

You may have noticed your spouse clench his or her hands whenever you are trying to convince her to do something she is not willing to do; here, their clenched hands tell you how frustrated they are with you.

## Rubbing Hands

This hand gesture indicates excitement. Whenever you are super-excited about something imminent, you are likely to rub your hands. For instance, the time you knew your father was buying you a bicycle, or when you and your best friend were making hiking plans, you may have unconsciously rubbed your hands together.

## Pointing Fingers

Pointing your finger at someone is an authoritative gesture. You usually make this gesture when you are imposing yourself on others. Pointing a finger at someone shows arrogance and anger towards a person. People often point finger at others when insulting them or with the intent is to make someone feel inferior.

When you become angry during a conversation, you start pointing fingers at the person you are talking to as a gesture to show your authority. Apart from pointing a finger at others, many point fingers in the air. They do so to emphasize their point during a conversation and to exhibit their confidence. You may have seen preachers and politicians make this gesture when emphasizing a point.

## Hands on Heart

This hand and arm gesture shows sincerity and affection. It indicates you are speaking directly from your heart. If someone wants to convince you he or she is not lying to you and is completely honest about a topic, he or she will place his or her hand(s) on heart.

## Hands behind Your Back

This gesture is common among men. Keeping your hands behind your back shows your level of confidence because having your hands behind the back exposes your front body and you do not fidget. Sometimes, this gesture shows respect for someone.

For instance, when talking to your boss (especially if you greatly respect your boss or perceive him/her as an authority figure), you are likely to place your hands behind your back.

All these unconscious gestures form different forms of body language indicating your hidden emotions and feelings. Some unconscious gestures or facial expressions directly link to a thought pattern. If you identify them, you can unlock anyone's mind.

To explain this notion better, here is an example of poker. Poker has a great involvement of facial expressions and hand movement. The unconscious gestures exhibited by a player can act as a hint for others to understand a player's next move. Touching the face is a common gesture used by players when they are bluffing. If you know what this gesture means, you can counter bluff.

Another important element of body language is speech recognition. Let us deeply explore this factor.

## Speech Pattern Recognition

A person's tone speaks volumes about the person's mood and feelings. Voice is an important part of our personality; it shows our age, gender, and few personality traits. Even a single word you speak is enough to express the excitement, sadness, or confusion in your voice.

You may have noticed the different tonal changes that occur in your tone during the day. The change of your tone depends on the person you are talking to or the kind of message you are trying to convey.

If you meet an old friend after ages, your voice becomes louder or shriller than normal because it is full of excitement. If you are upset, your voice becomes harsh.

The changes in your tone clearly express the changes in your moods, emotions, and feelings.

To understand people better, you need to understand the kind of tone they use. The best way to understand different tones is by using yourself as an example. This way, you will realize the change in your voice due to change in moods or emotions.

Read the following types of tones and relate them with the tones you use every day.

**Speaking Plainly**

When nothing exciting is going on in your life, you talk with a plain voice that hardly shows any emotion. If someone talks to you with a plain voice, it means the person is bored with his or her life or bored with you.

## Sarcastic Tone

We use a sarcastic tone to taunt a person.

A stressful situation can also make your tone sarcastic showing your frustration. For instance, if you are running for president at your college, you are likely to talk to your competitor in a sarcastic tone.

## Suspenseful Tone

People often speak with the element of suspense in their tone to make the conversation sound more exciting and to gain the listener's attention. They do this by taking sudden pauses and controlling the rise and fall of the voice. With the suspense element in your voice, a boring talk can become interesting.

## Sad Tone

When people talk in a slow and low voice, it shows their resentment and sadness about something. If you are talking to a friend who talks slowly with a low voice, it means something is bothering him and he feels sad.

## Excited Tone

A voice filled with excitement shows your enthusiasm and happiness about something. When you are doing something exciting such as going to a fun filled event or meeting an old friend, your voice will be excited. When you are very excited, you tend to speak loudly and quickly in a single breath.

While noticing the tone of your voice, it is also important to analyze its pace so you can better understand people's emotions.

## Notice the Pace of the Voice

The pace at which you speak reveals your level of confidence or nervousness. For example, when you converse with a very confident person, you will notice self-assurance in the person's voice; the person is likely to speak slowly and clearly taking small pauses, making sure you understand and follow the conversation.

Take your boss as an example. Your boss probably delivers his/her thoughts and ideas in a low pace with strong voice making sure he/she is loud and clear and everyone can easily understand his/her points. The pace of his/her voice and his/her tone of voice clearly exhibit high self-confidence.

On the other hand, if you talk to someone who lacks self-belief, that person's speech will be hushed and hurried to display lack of self-confidence.

## Use of Words and Their Repetition

After learning about the different tones as well as what they mean, you should now focus on the words a person uses. The words a person uses depict the thoughts going inside the person's mind. The kind of words a person uses to express him or herself shows that person's thoughts about the people and things around him or her.

For example, if your friend constantly praises himself or uses good words to describe his personality, then you will understand the amount of respect he has for himself.

Let us look at another example of your neighbor who uses the word 'I' in every conversation. This means your neighbor focuses more on herself or she is a self-centered person who only loves talking about herself.

Sometimes, the people you talk to continuously talk about the same topic or repeatedly use specific words. This indicates their attention is somewhere else. For instance, if you are talking with your sister and she repeatedly talks about the fight she had in school, this is your cue to understand how angry she is and her attention remains focused on that incident.

A common reason why most people learn how to analyze people is to detect their lies. As such, we need to explain how you can use body language and facial expressions to detect a liar and a dishonest person.

# A Bit About Lie Detection

Lie detection boils down to noticing the inconsistencies in what someone is saying verbally and what someone is projecting through body language or nonverbal cues. Lie detection involves critically observing a person's facial expression, body language, and gestures.

Nonverbal cues are the most reliable ways to detect lies because no matter how hard you try to lie, your body unconsciously signals what it feels.

## Lie Detection through the Eyes

You can easily tell what a person is thinking by looking into his or her eyes. When a left-handed person tells a lie, his or her eyes will move upwards towards the left. This eye movement indicates they are visualizing or inventing a response, rather than remembering one. The opposite is true for right-handed people. While detecting lies through someone's eyes, remember the following points.

## 1: Watch the Eyelids

If someone closes his or her eyelids for a long time, it means the person is trying to avoid eye contact. If the person blinks more than 3 times, it is a sign of nervousness and apprehension that you will catch him or her. If someone uses the hands to cover his or her eyes, this is yet another sign that the person wants to 'block out' the truth.

## 2; Pointing of Eyes

Our eyes point at things we find attractive or where our body wants to go. If you are talking to someone who is lying, the person will continuously look at the door or watch signaling the desire to cut short the conversation because the person is fearful you will catch the lie.

## 3: Avoiding Eye Contact

Breaking eye contact is the most basic way to identify a lie. Someone who has complete confidence about what he or she is saying will never avoid eye contact. However, if someone is lying, he or she will definitely avoid eye contact.

## 4: Facial Expressions

Observing facial expressions can help you detect a lie. The most common facial expressions observed in a liar are, dilated pupil, the appearance of lines on the forehead, narrowing of the eyebrows, and blinking eyes. Sweat on the forehead and an angry expression are common with these facial expressions.

## 5: Dilated Pupils

Pupil dilation indicates tension and concentration. When someone gets worried about exposure, the pupils unconsciously dilate as the person thinks of ways to hide the lie. If you are talking to someone but you are unsure if the person is honest or not, look at the person's pupils for answers.

## Lines on Forehead

Someone who is lying will definitely have lines on the forehead because of the stress the person has to bear as he/she seeks ways to cover the lie.

Apart from the facial expression, we can also observe many other gestures in a liar.

## Clearing of Throat

If someone is lying to you, he or she will probably clear his or her throat more than once as a nervous gesture due to stress.

## Backward Head Movement

When someone is telling a lie, the head always moves backwards. This gesture occurs as the lying person tries to avoid the source of anxiety because people tend to distance themselves from things they dislike.

## Hard Swallowing

Because the throat of someone who is lying becomes immediately dry, the person swallows hard to bring moisture back to avoid clearing his throat. This is common in people trying to hide their lying.

## Statement Analysis to Determine Lie

Analyzing someone's lie through his or her statement is the last step in lie detection. Sometimes what people say does not support their body language. This allows you to detect lies. People often stammer or talk at a fast pace as a way of trying to avoid lie discovery.

For instance, if you suspect your classmate stole your money, and when you ask her about it, you notice darting eyes, nervousness in her tone, and her body language does not support her statement that she did not steal the money, it means she is lying and has stolen it or knows who did.

No matter how good a person is at lying, if the person's body language is not supportive of his or her statement, that person is lying. To identify a liar, analyze someone's body language and determine if it matches with the person's statement. If the two contradict, you have a liar on your hands.

You now have a complete idea on how to analyze your target by studying body language, expressions, and gestures. This was just one way to analyze people. If you wish to analyze people more efficiently then you need a framework to analyze all the information obtained from the target's body language and expressions.

# Conclusion

Congratulations! You now have a framework you can use to be able to analyze people effectively and gain an in-depth understanding of their personality. Your careful observations will allow you to influence people more easily, as well as giving you an insight into their psychology and decision making process.

You have also learned how to analyze body language by observing their facial expressions, their gestures, and their verbal tonality. Using the information contained in this book, you will easily read the people around you like open books themselves!

The best way to increase your ability to analyze people is to practice the information in this book. Over time, you will develop your abilities and become adept at reading between the lines and understanding the psychology of others. As mentioned previously, this single ability can become your greatest asset in areas of business, relationships, and self improvement.

Don't forget to subscribe to the

Modern Psychology Publishing newsletter

Be the first to receive information about new book releases, free promotions, and the latest news to help guide you on your journey of mastering your psychology!

Made in the USA
Lexington, KY
26 April 2017